German U-I Type XXI

Bergen, Norway, Spring 1945: Three Type XXI U-boats, ready for service, wait for action. An older boat has tied up outside.

Siegfried Breyer

Schiffer Military/Aviation History
Atglen, PA

Bibliography (Selected)

Author group, Technikmuseum "Wilhelm Bauer", Bremerhaven 1990.

Berezhnoy, Trofei i Reparatsii VMF SSSR, Yakutsk 1994.

Breyer & Koop, Die Schiffe und Fahrzeuge der deutschen Bundesmarine 1956-76, Munich 1978 (new edition 1996).

Fock, Flottenchronik, Hamburg 1995

———, Kampfschiffe—Marinenschiffbau auf deutschen Werften 1870 bis heute, Hamburg 1995

Gabler, Unterseebootbau, Koblenz 1987.

Gröner, Die deutschen Kriegsschiffe 1815-1945, Vol. 3, Koblenz 1985.

Köhl, Vom Original zum Modell, Uboottyp XXI, Koblenz 1988.

Rössler, Uboottyp XXI, Koblenz 1986.

———, Geschichte des deutschen Ubootbaus, Vol. 2, Koblenz 1987.

———, Die deutschen Uboote und ihre Werften, Koblenz 1990.

Rohwer, Uboote—eine Chronik in Bildern, Oldenburg 1962.

——— & Himmelchen, Chronology of the War at Sea 1939-1945, London 1992.

Tarrant, Das letzte Jahr der Kriegsmarine, Wölfersheim-Berstadt 1996.

Photo Credits

Listed here are those sources of photographs which were available for use in this volume. In many (in fact, most) cases, though, it is no longer possible to determine the actual origin, and for that reason the secondary sources (such as collections) must be stated, or the general or suspected origin.

Federal Archives, Koblenz (15); Bibliothek für Zeitgeschichte, Stuttgart (12); Bundesmarine (2); Breyer Collection (19); Gröner Collection (1), Lemachko Collection (1); Possmann (1); Royal British Navy (1); Swedish Navy (4).

All drawings are copyrighted by S. Breyer.

Cover artwork by Steve Ferguson, Colorado Springs, CO.

Translated from the German by Ed Force

Printed in China.
ISBN: 0-7643-0787-8

This book was originally published under the title,
Marine Arsenal-Wunderwaffe Elektro-Uboot Typ XXI
by Podzun-Pallas Verlag.

We are interested in hearing from authors with book ideas on related topics.

Foreword

For a long time we have taken it for granted—the big, fast U-boat of our age, nuclear powered and able to stay under the surface of the water for weeks, even months if necessary. And yet, scarcely more than forty years have passed since the first nuclear-powered submarine, the American Nautilus, gained worldwide attention on its maiden voyage and introduced a new era in naval warfare. But who recalls that about fifty years have passed since a U-boat design appeared that was technically somewhat less staggering but just as revolutionary for its time in terms of effects and potentialities? This was the Type XXI U-boat that appeared in the last phase of World War II, in which—at the "last minute", so to speak—one of the many proclaimed "wonder weapons" came on the scene to strengthen the German will to presevere.

The prescribed size of this book required concentration on the essential: it is self-evident that much more could have been presented on this subject. Whole books have been written about it already; the most important and most thorough are those by Rössler and Köhl (see the bibliography)—and there is nothing to be added to these books. This volume is presented, reporting as completely as possible and as concisely as necessary about this development.

Many readers will take particular pleasure in finding that—for the first time in specialist literature!—it has become possible to offer a precise reference to those Type XXI boats that fell into Soviet hands at the war's end. The result is very much more modest than had previously been considered possible—for very little could be done about these units. The few who were involved with them in active service all retired from service just ten years after the end of the war!

Published by Schiffer Publishing Ltd.
4880 Lower Valley Road
Atglen, PA 19310
Phone: (610) 593-1777
FAX: (610) 593-2002
E-mail: Schifferbk@aol.com
Please visit our web site catalog at www.schifferbooks.com
or write for a free catalog.
This book may be purchased from the publisher.
Please include $3.95 postage.
Try your bookstore first.

Pre-History

After the German U-boat weapon had scored numerous sinkings in 1941-42, its numbers of successful sinkings receded almost alarmingly in 1943. At the same time, it suffered more and more losses; most of the boats were hit while on the surface—often quite surprisingly, "out of a clear blue sky", as it were—by long-range aircraft, which the Allied had applied in ever-increasing numbers over their areas of operation and approach routes. The reasons for this change in the "Battle of the Atlantic" resulted from progress in the enemy's surveillance technology. With the constant spread of radar reconnaissance, the German U-boats lost the most important conditions for successful operation, namely the element of surprise.

As is known, the principle of radar surveillance is based on the use of very short electric waves, which are reflected when they meet with a solid object. Since this process can also be operated from the air, and thus from aircraft, the area under surveillance could be enlarged very greatly, and naturally beyond the surveillance range of escort vehicles, which by nature were very limited in range anyway. The use of this process allowed the convoy ships and their securing powers to be warned systematically of approaching u-boats, so that the convoys could withdraw and the sub-chasing forces could be deployed against them. Once sighted, it usually took only a short time before the enemy defense began, so that the U-boats were forced to dive, and these conditions made German U-boat operations more and more difficult. When underwater, the U-boats' radius of action was by nature very limited. For the Type VII C boats—the usual mainstays of the German U-boat war—the radius of action was only about 80 nautical miles at a speed of only four knots. But they could not recharge either their batteries or their compressed-air tanks that fast—and thus they faced a dilemma: their chances of attacking decreased in these changed conditions, while their losses and risks increased.

The measures that were taken against the enemy surveillance techniques were all more or less improvised and not at all suited to restore the U-boat war to its old style. To be sure, the U-boats received a device by which they were warned (if there was time) and could dive as soon as they were picked up by enemy radar. But then, under the surface of the water, they lacked the most important prerequisite for attacking: "sight". Every warship that was given the designation of "U-boat" at that time really did not deserve it, for it was nothing but a warship for operations **above** water, which only occasionally—for tactical reasons—was supposed to dive and hide itself. But then it was slow, blind, ponderous and thus robbed of its attacking strength.

Purely in theory, the battery-powered electric motors allowed a top speed of some five to seven knots, but only for a few hours, since the batteries were exhausted very soon. But then it was time to surface, so the batteries could be recharged. Doing this required the running of the Diesel engines, which naturally meant a steady discharge of exhaust gases. In view of the nearly gapless radar surveillance in the area of operations, no commander could dare any longer to exhaust the batteries of his craft by overly extended underwater cruising, for he constantly had to reckon on having to surface in an area not free of enemies and thereby running the risk of being spotted and pursued. Of necessity, then, there was only one course: moving slowly under the surface of the water, at some two or three, or at most four, knots—any more could have been fatal. But thus there was scarcely the possibility any longer of attacking enemy shipping unless the ships had approached it—but this was very rarely the case. For even a convoy, the speed of which necessarily is that of its slowest ship, usually trav-

A Type VII C boat on the surface in the Arctic. This picture was taken in a sector of the war in which U-boats could remain on the surface without being spotted and attacked by the enemy as soon as they surfaced.

eled at a speed of seven to ten knots. Once taken under the surface, a U-boat of the types then in use could only rarely launch an attack.

This dramatic development did not come as a complete surprise to the German command—on the contrary, it had cast its shadow for months already, leading up to the "Black May" of the war year 1943, in which 41 U-boats were lost. To the same degree as the German command made efforts to throw more U-boats into the "Battle of the Atlantic", the other side increased its efforts to become the master of this situation which could have been fatal in the end. In the entire year of 1940, the German Navy had lost 22 U-boats, in 1941 they lost 35, and even in the first half of 1942 the losses were still within bearable limits when one considers that more U-boats were being sent to the front constantly. But beyond the middle of that year it became clear that the other side had the advantage: in the entire war year of 1942, 85 U-boats were lost, 53 of them in the last six months. The German command saw that it was faced with one of the most serious problems of the war to date.

A way out of this dilemma appeared in the development of the "Walter U-boat" 1*, which had already begun before the war began, though even now it could not be determined when the U-boat would be ready for service at the front. With it, a true revolutionizing of the U-boat war would have been attainable, for it had overcome the weaknesses of the previous U-boats: it moved fast underwater and created much less exhaust. But in view of the increasingly threatening situation, Doenitz, in command of the Navy since the beginning of 1943, did not want to wait for its readiness to see service. It was simply too late to give up the U-boat war and replace it with a different kind of naval warfare—if indeed there had been such an alternative for the Navy. Just in view of the increasingly large deliveries of war materials across the Atlantic from the USA to the European allies, the U-boat had to remain the single effective weapon with which to combat the enemy. Every ton of these war materials had its effect on the land fronts against the German troops, who had long since lost the offensive advantage and had to wage an increasingly difficult defensive war against the much stronger enemy. If their burdens were to be lightened, it could be done only through the U-boat war.

---

1. The "Walter U-boat", so named after Professor Helmuth Walter (1900-1980), who directed the development of a new and different propulsion system for U-boats, was supposed to bring a change in the U-boat war. It was a unified system which used hydrogen peroxide (H_2O_2) in concentration up to 90%. In addition to the advantage of a drive nearly independent of outside air, the boat was also supposed to attain a considerably higher underwater speed than had been possible before.

"Seeing" was just as important to a U-boat's success as it was to the boat's survival. In order to enlarge its field of vision, tests were made with a sighting place mounted on "stilts", as seen here on a Type VII boat. One certainly could have seen farther in clear weather, but the experiment was not successful.

In order to fight back against the greatly increasing danger from the air, the AA armament of the U-boats was much strengthened. To be sure, they did succeed in shooting down some enemy planes, but the danger was not lessened; on the contrary, it increased more.

Above: When the war began, international law was still obeyed in the U-boat war. But when the British Admiralty ordered the arming of merchant vessels, the scene changed. Still, German U-boat crews rescued a number of survivors. When the enemy's opposition became ever stronger, the order was given not to attempt rescues, so as not to fall victim oneself. As of 1943, no U-boat could still afford to take such a risk. Two years earlier—as seen here from U 124—this was still quite possible.

The U-boats returning from missions, often very successful ones, were always welcomed heartily at their support points. The longer the war lasted, the fewer boats came back, and the numbers of ships sunk by them likewise diminished. This signaled that the earlier U-boat had lost its reason for existence.

Above: As of 1942, there were more cases in which enemy aircraft attacked quite unexpectedly, and there was no time for self-defense. Then the U-boats lay helpless in the hail of bombs and bullets, and no longer had a chance. The Anglo-American forces owed this success to their advanced radar technology.

Left: The return from a mission became more and more a matter of chance, especially when—as can be seen here—a U-boat had suffered serious damage and was no longer able to dive.

The Birth of the Type XXI U-boat

In view of this highly alarming situation, waiting for the "Walter U-boats" to be developed fully for front-line service could not be accepted; rather it was absolutely necessary to act at once. At this time a leading member of the "Walter U-boat" project, Dipl.-Ing. Heep, got the idea that it might be possible to equip the Type XVIII "Walter U-boat, essentially finished, intended for future front service and designed for speed, with a standard but much more powerful Diesel-electric powerplant and thus to bring new life to the U-boat war. This idea was taken up by the Naval Building Director Oelfken, a senior member of the bureau responsible for U-boat development at the main office for warship construction. He arrived at a positive result, which he summarized in brief as follows: "If we want to build such a large boat and have so much space available, we can also accomplish very much more than before with the conventional powerplant. When there is also much more emphasis placed on the underwater characteristics than on surface characteristics, then we can naturally design a conventional powerplant differently than in the past.[1] Therefore he recommended building a boat based on the Type XVIII, with good hydronamic form and a lack of emphasis on special seaworthiness for surface cruising. Two qualities, namely a greater diving time limit and a sufficient operational underwater speed, were decisive. This decision was agreed to by Doenitz—meanwhile promoted to Grand Admiral and Commander of the Navy. The work began at once; it resulted in the now-legendary Type XXI U-boat, which was subsequently referred to often as the "Great Electroboat". Its existence is attributable to the ideas of the "civilians" Heep and Oelfken.

---

1. Quoted from Rössler, Geschichte des deutschen Ubootbaus, Vol. 2, p. 339.

U 793 was one of the first experimental U-boats for the revolutninary but not yet service-ready Walter powerplant, independent of outside air. Readiness for the front was still some distance away in April 1944, when U 793 left the Hamburg shipyards (above).

*U 1407 belonged to a second series of U-boats with the Walter system. It survived the war and came into British hands. As the **Meteorite**, it was used by the Royal Navy for testing purposes for some years.*

The Project Becomes Reality

When the designs for the Type XXI—which included about 18,400 individual drawings and more than 6200 parts lists—were prepared in such a short time that they could be presented on June 19, 1943, this indicates a high degree of effort on the part of all participants, such as normally would never have been possible, and was explainable only because of the war situation. In particular, it was Doenitz himself who immediately recognized the advantages of the new type and had given a green light for its realization. Thereby he hoped to be able to resume the collapsed U-boat war and to deliver severe blows to the enemy's shipping of materials vital for life and warfare once again. In fact, the new boats seemed to be able to fulfill the hopes that were incorporated in them. They were to carry three times as many batteries as the earlier boats; the hull and conning tower were extensively streamlined in order to reduce the water resistance to the lowest possible amount. The underwater speed was to reach 17 knots—an almost unimaginably high speed at that time! And there was even more: With completely new orientation devices, the boats were supposed to be capable of attacking while underwater and firing their torpedoes from the depths only on the basis of bearings. The length of a dive should be extendable as desired by means of the air mast, the so-called "snorkel". Of course, the air mast was nothing new in U-boat design. Its idea is almost as old as man's conception of diving itself (even the Hollanders had experimented successfully with it in the years between the two world wars and tested a workable design, the so-called "snuifer"). In other navies, though, the snorkel had been forgotten again, because it did not have any practical applications at that time; Germany was first to take up this idea again in its time of need.

The snorkel is a hydraulically extendable mastlike double pipe of steel, which connects the inside of the boat with the atmospheric air. It consists of an exhaust pipe, which is linked to the Diesel engines, and an air intake which ends free in the inside of the boat. At the upper end, the snorkel is held open by a floating valve; when underwater, this closes automatically and thus prevents sea water from entering. With the help of the snorkel, the U-boat could run at periscope depth at about six knots and charge its batteries at the same time. The inconspicuous snorkel head either avoided enemy radar sighting altogether or limited it to a scarcely noticeable minimum. Of course in the daytime—on a calm sea—the snorkel head can be seen optically, for it causes a clearly visible trail of bubbles trailing behind it. The most suitable time to use the snorkel was therefore the night. To be sure, individual U-boats of all types had been

The Type XXI U-boats could only bring new life to the U-boat war if they could go into action in large numbers. Therefore other measures had to be taken to attain this goal. Construction by earlier shipbuilding methods—as here with a pressure-hull segment of a Type VII C boat—was completely unsuitable.

fitted with a snorkel, but this alone was naturally not sufficient to give the boats back the potency of their earlier attacking power. With it, they were better able to escape from pursuit, but they had to remain blind and slow beneath the surface. In the new U-boats, though, this was no longer the case. By their very nature, they provided new and different characteristics and capabilities, with which the snorkel could now be used effectively.

Over time, 740 boats in all were contracted for, of which there were on the following dates:

November 6, 1943: 290 boats

May 6, 1944: 278 boats

September 27, 1944: 172 boats

It was hoped that the first of them would be ready for action in the summer of 1944, so that sooner or later a new life could be given to the U-boat war.

Sektion ⑨

Sektion ⑤ₐ

The sections of the XXI U-boat, with pressurized hull shown in heavy lines and shadings.

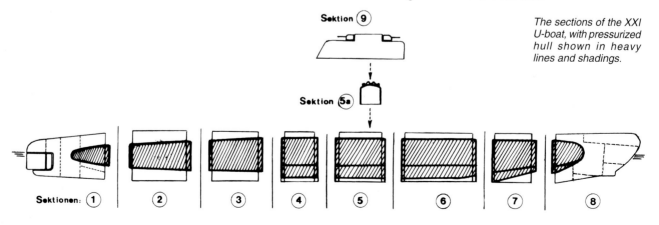

Sektionen: ① ② ③ ④ ⑤ ⑥ ⑦ ⑧

Above: This shows the raw pressure-hull segments as delivered by the steel companies. Many of these raw segments had been stored in Germany and were discarded after the war ended. These here were rebuilt by a Frankfurt apple-wine brewery into tanks for their product.

Left: Section 6 of a Type XXI U-boat, clearly showing the outside braces and the cross-section somewhat resembling a figure 8.

New Means of Mass Production

At this point in time, the vast number of new U-boats could be achieved only through energetic measures in the entire armament industry. In order to carry out the program as quickly as possible, warship building, thus including the designing and building of the new boats, was turned over to the so-called "Hauptausschuss Schiffbau" (HAS) of the Armament Ministry. The Navy decided on this noteworthy measure only after much thought; but it was put aside deliberately because in the tense situation of the wartime economy, better deliveries for U-boat building, especially in view of the difficulties of motor delivery, were promised by making warship building part of the responsibility of the Armament Ministry.

Naturally, the building methods also had to be changed; the former shipbuilding methods could scarcely be considered any more, what with the markedly longer times involved. Therefore the HAS introduced the so-called "Sektionsbau" (section building, also called "Schussbau") as the factory production method; it consisted every boat being divided into the same number of sections, and every section—each independently of the others—being completely finished by itself. Each of the nine shipbuilding yards—which were in turn dependent on 33 supplying firms—built only up to four sections, thus always using the same components. The finished sections of a group of shipyards were then transported to one of the three assembly yards, where the boats were assembled and completed. All the design work was carried out by a central office, the "Ingenieurbüro Glückauf" (IBG), which was located in Blankenburg in the Harz Mountains. The IBG made the necessary supplies available to all the shipyards and suppliers, coordinated the workn and supervised and directed the deliveries of materials.

As calculated, by this method only 266,000 work hours per boat should be required as a final target, and according to the following calculations:

Rolling the steel and delivery for steel construction: 16 days

Construction and production of raw sections:	40 days
Transport for section building:	5 days
Equipping sections at the shipyard:	50 days
Transport to assembly shipyard:	4 days
Assembly on the slipway:	50 days
Equipping after launching:	6 days
Shipyard testing:	5 days
Total:	176 days

From the autumn of 1944 on, a monthly production of 35 U-boats was planned, but this was, of course, far from reality.

The planned 266,000 work hours were never attained; in December 1944, 332,500 hours per boat still had to be expended. This was clearly more than had to be applied to all the Type VII C boats. In the autumn of 1943, 220,000 to 260,000 work hours had been required. If the planned goal could not be attained, it was primarily because of the constantly increasing air raids on Germany and German-occupied territory. This, of course, struck the shipyards themselves more rarely, but it took an increasing greater toll on the material situation and the supply system. All the conditions included in the plans were ruined by the development of the war.

The pressure hulls of the Type XXI U-boats were made in eight sections, with two or three sections built exclusively by the assembly shipyards, which were:

Blohm & Voss, Hamburg

A.G. "Weser", Bremen

Friedrich Schichau, Fanzig

The other sections were transported from the construction yards to the assembly yards on waterways or railways. They were stored there for a short time, standing outdoors in columns, until they were assembled.

The sections brought in by special means of transport—none of them had a weight of more than 200 tons—were then set on the blocks and joined together by means of electric welding and then moved off, for right behind them the first sections of the next U-boats were being prepared and the next sections were being brought in. So there was on all the slipways—often occupied by three or four U-boats—an active process of new construction, assembly and launching. Every time the foremost boat was launched, the sections of the following boat were pushed forward and a new boat begun behind it. In the construction basin, only the remaining work was done, and after a boat was equipped, it was tested without delay.

Of course, this decentralization made every shipyard dependent on the others. If one shipyard was crippled temporarily by an air raid, then the production of the entire group had to be interrupted.[2]* Thus the building of sections proved to be very prone to disturbances; when it could be carried out at all, it was because the enemy air raids on the shipyards, at least in the war year of 1944, were no longer carried out with the usual intensity. Obviously the Allies had not yet fully recognized the danger that threatened them with the new U-boats, or they had estimated it incorrectly, perhaps only because they depended on their highly developed radar technology in attacking German U-boats.

Another problem area was engine production. Here the building of sections could do nothing to help. One had to get by with a type of engine that had been developed for the earlier types of U-boats. This was cut down from nine to six cylinders, with the compression simultaneously increased, so that 90 v.H., the power of the nine-cylinder engine, was still attained; the lower compression of the nine-cylinder motors had been chosen for the sake of operating reliability, which was now necessarily put at risk by the adaptation.

---

2. This had also been recognized soon by the German leadership. For this reason, they planned and built, beginning in 1943, a gigantic bomb-safe production bunker at Bremen-Farge, but this building was never finished.

Above: This section—already fitted with an outer hull—is finished and is moved by a crane. This is section 3, one of those located abaft the turret.

Left: The section 5 of a Type XXI U-boat, seen when nearly finished, also fitted with an outer hull. In the background is the bow section of another boat.

The installation of the starboard Diesel engine in section 3. The port engine is already mounted.

Another view of the installation of a Diesel engine in section 3. This is U-3001, which was assembled at the Deschimag shipyard in Bremen.

Above and right: Sections ready for assembly in Hamburg.

The bow sections of two Type XXI U-boats. The torpedo openings of the boat in back are already closed; the one in front still lacks its doors. In both, the hydrodynamically designed "balcony" device, which enclosed the receivers of the underwater mistening apparatus, can be seen clearly.

These unfinished Type XXI U-boats are seen in the Deschimag shipyard in Bremen just after the end of the war. The boats are at various stages of completion.

Below: A look at the large slipways at Blohm & Voss in Hamburg, occupied with several Type XXI U-boats.

A section of a Type XXI U-boat on the slipway, seen directly from the front. This is U-3001, which was assembled at the Deschimag shipyard in Bremen.

U-3001 again; in front of section C is one of the two Diesel engines, ready to be moved in and installed.

Left: A Type XXI (stern) section, seen at the Deschimag shipyard in Bremen, with a section 2 behind it.

U-2502 in a dock for examination after being taken to Great Britain. The side rudder, the rear pair of depth rudders and the two three-bladed propellers can be seen clearly.

Below: The Blohm & Voss shipyards just after the war ended. Here the rear of a Type XXI U-boat is ready to be assembled.

The Technology of the New Y-boat Type

If we take a close look at a Type XXI U-boat, then the external departure from the shape of all previously built German U-boats catches our eye at once. It shows a much more favorable shape than before. This can be explained by the fact that all previous U-boats were designed as surface craft, meaning that they were so designed that they could reach their highest possible marching speed on the surface, since a high speed was disregarded for their more or less short-term diving travel, for the reason that the available electrical energy would not have sufficed for a longer stay underwater. The new boats, on the other hand, were capable of attaining a higher cruising speed underwater than on the surface, thanks to their hydrodynamically advantageous design and their greater battery capacity. For this, of course, some of the special characteristics of a surface ship had to be sacrificed. The lower length-to-width ratio (11.6, as opposed to 10.8 in the Type VII C boats) certainly allowed higher speeds underwater, but at the cost of maneuverability on the surface. Therefore much skill in seamanship was required to maneuver these boats in harbors or narrow waterways. For this reason, towing was always called for when entering or leaving harbors or maneuvering.

The pressure hull was divided into seven watertight sections; in cross-section it resembled a number 8 standing on its head, for under the larger pressure hull was a smaller one, extending about one third of the boat's length. It was separated from the upper pressure hull by a strong deck and served primarily to carry some of the considerably more numerous batteries. The use of external braces also guaranteed a more favorable utilization of space as well as quicker production. It goes without saying that electric welding was used in all the assembly. Another novelty in German U-boat building was the location of the front depth rudder **above** water, as well as being capable of being turned inward, like those of several foreign navies; this had the effect of not exposing it unnecessarily to the action of the sea. A pair of large horizontal fins were located at the stern, extending considerably beyond the width of the boat. Out of these fins there projected the propeller shafts, which diverged more in the Type XXI boat than in any previously developed German U-boat. This was so because, with the spindle shape of the new boats and their conically tapering hulls, the engine units had to be mounted close beside each other. The fins gave the shafts the necessary stability when they came out of the pressure hull. Their replaceable valves served to protect the propellers when opening or closing. The shape and attachment of the side rudder also differed from all that had gone before. In front, under the bow, was the so-called "balcony listening device", which ended in a cupola shape at the back. Probably the most visible external feature of the Type XXI boats was their longer and more streamlined tower, with its two small anti-aircraft gun turrets at the end positions. Such a completely closed tower shape had never been seen on German U-boats before! It

was originally intended to arm each of these anti-aircraft turrets with one 30 mm twin Flak gun, for which a development contract had been issued to Rheinmetall in 1942. Since this could not be finished at the right time, 20 mm twin guns were installed instead. The Flak guns were a typical leftover from those years when a U-boat could still fight against a single enemy plane with a good hope of success. But now, what with radar surveillance from the air, the only effective protection for a U-boat against aircraft was the command to "dive fast", if it could still be given and it was not already too late for it (but then the anti-aircraft weapons could no longer be used). With this in mind, it is doubtful whether these weapons ever could have been used successfully in battle. For that reason, they ultimately add up to an actually unneeded amount of weight. They could, of course, be operated by a hydraulically powered system from inside the boat, so that the operating personnel would be relatively safe from the enemy's use of on-board weapons. In practice, though, this weapon system proved to be rather complicated, as well as sensitive to disturbances, and it also had little resistance to the pressure waves of underwater explosions, like those of water bombs. A lot of hydraulic power was used in the Type XXI U-boats as a means of saving electrical energy—to a much greater degree than in the earlier boats: for the side rudders, the depth rudder and the torpedo-tube flaps, the periscope and the snorkel.

Out of the tower there rose two periscopes and one snorkel of the newest design. The last had been much improved from the systems of the earlier U-boats equipped with it. Unlike them, this had separate intake and exhaust masts, though linked together for deploying. Thus only one power source was needed for moving them up or down. For normal underwater cruising, the snorkel could be lowered to the extent that it was enclosed by the tower covering and thus did not cause any disturbance to the waterstream. The snorkel head was also fitted with a rubberlike, "waffled" camouflage mat ("chimney sweep"), which was made to absorb radar impulses. On it there was also a round dipole antenna for radar observation.

Aside from the cross-section structure of the pressure hull, it must be realized that its division—in principle—remained the same as on the older boats, but without the stern torpedo room that was practically obligatory. These and the possibility of firing at the enemy while departing had been given up. Instead, the bow torpedo weapon had been made stronger, in that—for the first time in the development of German U-boat design—six bow tubes had been installed. The bow room—and this too was new—now served exclusively as a torpedo room and no longer simultaneously as living quarters for the crew, as had been the case in all the older boats. In addition to the torpedoes in the tubes, 17 reserve torpedoes lay ready for use on side racks almost directly in front of the tubes. Ifin this situation one of the torpedoes in the tubes had to be serviced, then the reserve torpedo in front of that tube had to be placed on the deck. Under the pressure-hull deck, electrically pow-

Again we see U-2502 in a British dock; the picture was taken from a higher position and shows the complete boat, with its characteristic stern form easy to see.

ered trolleys, which ran on rails, were installed for charging or unloading the torpedoes.

With this fast loading apparatus, it should have been possible in combat to fire the first additional salvo in five to six minutes, and the second after about twenty minutes. Only on long missions was the total of 23 torpedoes not to be exhausted; in this case, only 20 torpedoes were planned for. It was also planned to carry twelve mines in place of four torpedoes, three of them carried per torpedo tube and fired by compressed air. But in none of these boats was the planned-for mine transport apparatus ever installed.

The powerplant differed greatly from all previous ones by producing almost 25 v.H. more for underwater use. For underwater cruising, two generators were on hand, built for the individual boats by the AEG, Brown Bovery & Cie., and Siemens-Schuckert firms. Each engine produced a maximum of 2500 PSe power; with them, a speed of 17.5 knots could be attained and sustained for about an hour, with slower speeds possible for correspondingly longer times. There were two electric motors, produced by Siemens-Schuckert, each producing 113 PSe and designed for "Schleichfahrt" or almost soundless running. They transmitted their power via wedge belts directly to the propeller shafts. At the lowest speed of 2 knots, the sound registered was zero; the highest speed still free of sound was 6 knots, and could be maintained for about 48 hours non-stop. Power for surface cruising and snorkel operation (as well as for charging the batteries) was provided by two MA four-stroke six-cylinder Diesel engines with blowers; the enfines produced 2000 PSe each. With them, a surface speed of 15.5 knots could be attained (compared to 17.5 knots by the Type VII C boats).

The living quarters of the new U-boats were far superior to those of the old boats. One section each afore and abaft the center was reserved almost completely for living quarters, and was kept as free as possible from passage through it. Bulks were erected, two and three high, numbering 49 in all and enough for the greater part of the crew. In other ways as well, relatively more comfort was offered here than had been, or could have been, the case previously. This was necessary, for the changed style of fighting was more of a threat to the crew, physically and psychologically, since the new boats were to operate underwater most of the time. Of course the oxygen for breathing was sufficient, but the saturation of the air with moisture, the changes in air pressure—usually when the snorkel was used—, the lack of ultra-violet rays, the loss of refreshment from fresh air, and many other problems had to be taken seriously. A radical solution was ruled out; the only thing that could be done was making the crew's life easier. This explains the frequent use of the word "comfort" in describing the living conditions.

Whereas attacking was formerly done with the help of the periscope, thus by means of optical observation, this process also changed in the new U-boat type: now a group of specially trained men worked at highly developed devices in the orientation room and gave out the coordinates for the attack. The nucleus of this equipment was the "balcony hearing device"; it picked up the propeller sounds of a convoy or fleet at greater distances than had previously been the case. The listening distances varied, of course, and depended on a number of incalculable factors (such as water level and temperature, salt content, etc.), but the enemy's course could at least be estimated fairly well.

Thereupon the attempt was made to steer the boat, thanks to its high underwater speed, onto a collision course and thus approach the enemy until it had come close. Then active orientation had to take over: the sending of impulses that—reflected by the underwater parts of the enemy ships— were picked up again and thus indicated direction and distance. The maximum range of this active orientation was then eight nautical miles. The enemy's direction and course were determined by short impulses, which were sent out according to a certain rhythm; the measuring precision of these impulses was approximately +/- 50 meters in distance and +/- 1 degree in direction.

This equipment, the most modern in any U-boat at that time, allowed the commander to attack solely on the basis of sound impulses; thereby he did not need to depend on the periscope, which could betray his position easily.

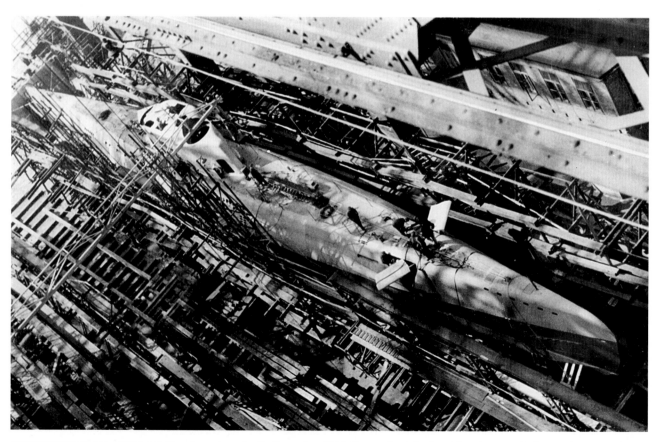

U 2537 on the slipway at Blohm & Voss. it was launched in December 1944. The two front depth rudders, here partly deployed, are easy to see.

U 2501 shortly before launching. The last jobs are being done on deck.

One of the Type XXI U-boats still on the slipway at Blohm & Voss in May 1945. The view goes from forward to aft. At the front of the tower is the still-empty opening for the forward 20 mm twin Flak guns.

The tower of U 2502. The number on its sides was not customary in the Navy; it was required by the British occupying forces to make the picture more meaningful.

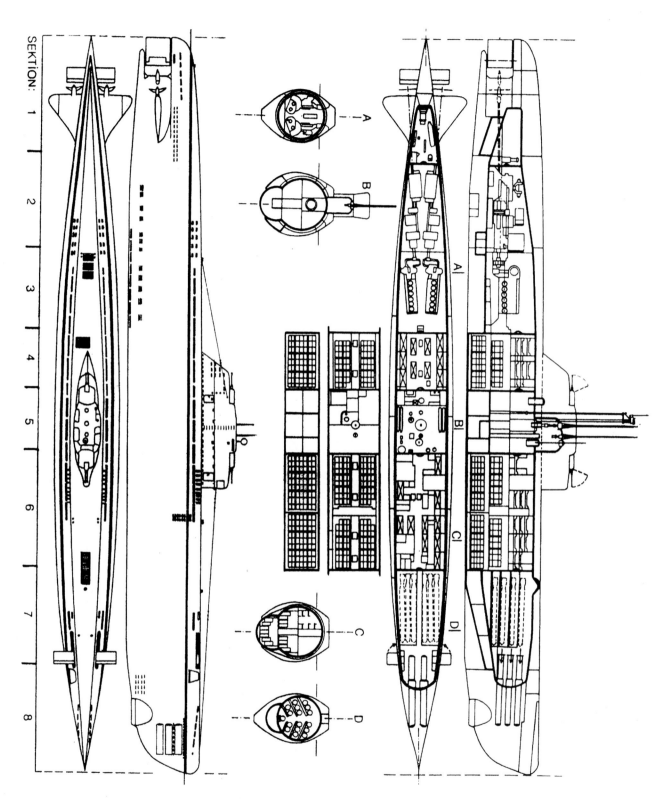

Drawing of the Type XXI U-boat. The letters indicate the positions of the cross-sections in the drawing.

Action and Results

Although this type arrived too late, one boat did have the chance to prove its special capabilities. It was U 2511, under the command of Corvette Captain Adalbert Schnee, who wore the oak leaves of the Knight's Cross, that left its Norwegian support base at Bergen on a mission late in April 1945. Having left the coastal waters, it immediately dived to advance underwater at normal marching speed into the western Atlantic, where it intended to attack convoys. Just one day later, near the east coast of Britain, it met a group of British sub-chasers; they spotted the boat, which was running normally at periscope depth, and immediately formed to attack. But U 2511 was not defenseless against them. With its orientation instruments it was able to follow the movements of its adversaries, get away from them and depart at high speed. And four days later, on May 4, 1945, it met a group of British warships, which included the cruiser **Norfolk** as well as destroyers. From the start, U 2511 was in such a favorable position that it only needed to make a slight change in its course to come directly into contact with the ships. Moving at soundless speed and not spotted by the British, the U-boat could make almost a textbook attack and get the cruiser directly in front of its torpedo tubes. . . but the commander did not give the command to fire, because—in view of the negotiations for Germany's capitulation—the Commander of U-boats had issued a general order not to attack. Thus U 2511 found itself once more on a return trip to Norway when this meeting took place. With strict accuracy, this was all recorded in the war diary, so that there could be no doubt about it.

It was a remarkable coincidence that there was aboard the **Norfolk** (which under other conditions would have become a certain victim of U 2511) an Admiralty commission whose special duty was to obtain information about the new U-boat type in Norway. And it was able to carry out this task, even though they did so—during the apparent attack—unknowingly. A few days after the capitulation, the commander of U 2511 met them on board and gave them detailed information. The Britons' first reaction was to regard his information as impossible, since not a single U-boat had been spotted by the orientation devices on the cruiser or its destroyer escort during the march. Only when they compared their own log books with the diary of U 2511 did it become clear to the British what a fate they had escaped . . . and from then on, the significance of this new German U-boat weapon was understood by the enemy.

The Type XXI U-boat was surely not a wonder weapon, as the Nazi propagandists wanted people to believe; rather it was a further development of the "Tauchboot", born of necessity, into the first "genuine" submarine. The Allies soon learned that these new U-boats had had great potential for giving the war at sea a new and different face if they had only been available sooner in considerable numbers. "Had the Germans been able to get the Type XXI to sea a year earlier, these submarines would probably have had a serious effect on our ability to keep our allies supplied with the necessary materials of war"—this was the judgment of an American naval officer four years after the end of the war.[1]

Even though this revolutionary new U-boat type could have no effect on the course and conclusion of the war—the handwriting on the wall said "too late!"—yet its influence on postwar submarine development was all the greater. It made clear that the U-boat as a weapon of war—which, in the Allied view, was seen as overcome toward the end of the war and thus lacking in any possible military uses that might be attempted—is yet not to be written off and, on the contrary, takes a role that must be rated more highly than ever before. Of all the victorious powers, the USA, Great Britain and the Soviet Union, and later France, gained the most profit from it. Their postwar submarine development was based solidly on the standard of the German Type XXI U-boat. Even though the nuclear-powered submarine entered into the picture of U-boat construction later, the non-nuclear submarines of our times are scarcely less effective, aside from the type armed with rockets. The beginning of it all was the German Type XXI U-boat—a perfectly straight line has led from it to the conventional submarines of today.

---

1. Lt. Commander A. N. Glennon, U.S. Navy, "The Weapon That Came Too Late", in "United States Naval Institute Proceedings", Vol. 187, No. 3, 1961.

U 3034 was one of the last Type XXI U-boats to be put into service. This took place on March 31, 1945 (this picture was taken shortly afterward); five weeks later the British marched into Bremen.

Opposite page: After the capitulation, this photograph was taken in a Norwegian harbor. From right to left are U 3515, U 3512, U 2518, U 2513, and (barely visible), U 2502. Note the extended snorkel mast of U 3512.

U 2501 before the west box of the "Elbe II" U-boat bunker at the Howaldt shipyard in Hamburg. On May 3, 1945 the boat was scuttled by its crew in this position. The picture was probably taken just before the boat was scuttled.

Building Contracts (issued or intended, including canceled)

Name	Contract Date	Shipyard	Total
U 2501-2631	11/6/1943	Blohm & Voss, Hamburg	131
U 2632-2762	5/6/1944	Blohm & Voss, Hamburg	119
U 3001-3088	11/6/1943	Deschimag, Bremen	88
U 3089-3100	5/6/1944	Deschimag, Bremen	12
U 3101-3176	5/6/1944	Bremer Vulkan Farge*	76
U 3177-3295	9/27/1944	Bremer Vulkan Farge*	119
U 3501-3571	11/6/1943	Schichau, Danzig	71
U 3572-3642	5/6/1944	Schichau, Danzig	71
U 3643-3695	9/27/1944	Schichau, Danzig	53
			740

* "Valentin" large bunker, not finished at war's end.

Manufacturers of Raw Sections

Section Number	Manufacturer
1	Hanneman & Co., Lübeck Norddeutscher Eisenbau, Sande bei Wilhelmshaven Gresse & Co., Wittenberg/Elbe Strassburger Werft, Strassburg-Neudorf
2	Gutehoffnungshütte, Oberhausen-Sterkrade Seibert, Aschaffenburg Dellschau, Berlin Eilers, Hannover
3	MAN, Mainz-Gustsvsburg Krupp-Stahlbau, Hannover Mittelstahl, Riesa Gollnow, Stettin
4	Fries-Sohn, Frankfurt/Main Hein, Lehmann & Co., Düsseldorf-Oberbilk Kelle & Hildebrandt, Dresden Gebrüder Heyking, Danzig
5	Krupp-Stahlbau, Rheinhausen Eggers & Co., Hamburg H.J. Jucho, Audorf bei Rendsburg August Klönne, Danzig
6	MAN, Hamburg Dortmunder Union (Werk Orange), Gelsenkirchen Demag, Bodenwerder Krupp-Druckenmüller, Stettin
7	Schäfer, Ludwigshafen Grohmann & Frosch, Wittenberg/Elbe Uebigau, Dresden Beuchelt & Co., Grünberg (Schlesien)
8	Hilgers AG, Rheinbrohl GHH Rheinwerft, Walsum Carl Später, Hamburg Beuchelt & Co., Grünberg (Sachsen)
9	Krupp

Size and Weight of Sections and where they were built

Number of section	Name	Length (meters)	Weight (tons)	Manufacturer
1	Heckraum	12.7	65	Howaldtswerke, Kiel, Danziger Werft
2	E-Maschinenraum	10.0	130	Kriegsmarinenwerft Wilhelmshaven, Danziger Werft
3	Dieselmotorenraum	8.4	140	Bremer Vulkan, Deutsche Werft Hamburg, Danziger Werft
4	Mannschaftsraum	5.	3 70	Deutsche Werft Hamburg, Flenderwerke Lübeck, Schichau Danzig
5	Zentrale, Kombüse, Hilfsmaschinen	7.6	140	Bremer Vulkan, Howaldtswerke Hamburg, Schichau Danzig
5a	Turm			
6	Vorderer Wohnraum	12.0	165	Bremer Vulkan, Deutsche Werft Hamburg, Deutsche Werft Gotenhafen
7		8.0	90	Deschimag Wesermünde, Deutsche Werke Gotenhafen
8	Torpedoraum	14.0	110	Deutsche Werke Kiel, Danziger Werft
9	Turmumbau	14.1	12	Blohm & Voss Hamburg, Deschimag Bremen, Schichau Danzig

Technical-tactical Data for U-boat Type XXI*

Outer Hull

Length overall	meters	76.70
Length on KWL	meters	75.40
Length on straight keel	meters	41.60
Width over [Mallkante]	meters	6.60
Width over stabilizing fins	meters	6.70**
Side height keel bottom-upper deck top	meters	7.70
Side height keel bottom-tower cover	meters	11.34

Pressure Hull

Length overall	meters	60.50
Diameter, upper pressure hull	meters	5.30
Diameter, lower pressure hull	meters	3.50
Pressure hull plate thickness	mm	26
Pressure hull volume	sq. m.	1150.70

Draught

Loaded boat: aft	meters	6.86
center	meters	6.32
forward	meters	5.77

Displacement

Displacement on surface	cubic meters	1621
Displacement underwater	cubic meters	1819
Official displacement underwater	cubic meters	2114
Dispmacement minus fuel and equipment	cubic meters	1280

* All data from Rössler a.a.O.
** To U 2539: 7.60 meters (planned: 8.00 meters)

Powerplants

For surface travel	two MAN 6-cylinder four-stroke Diesel engines, M6V 40/46, high compression (BBC-Büchi exhaust blower), power 2000 HP at 520 rpm each
For underwater travel	two SSW generators, 2 GU 365/30, with blowers, power 2500 HP at 1675 rpm each + two SSW generators, CV 323/28, power 113 HP at 350 rpm each (silent travel)
Batteries	six part batteries, 62 accucells each, (= 120 V) with 11,300 Ah with 20-hour discharging (cell weight 620 kg, total 230.64 tons)

Performance (Speed)

Surface travel (Diesel)	15.6 knots
Underwater (electric)	17.2 knots
Underwater (silent)	6.1 knots

Range at Sea

Maximum fuel supply	296.92 cubic meters
Surface travel (Diesel)	5100 nautical miles at 15.6 knots
	11150 nautical miles at 12.0 knots
	15500 nautical miles at 10.0 knots
	16500 nautical miles at 9.0 knots
Underwater (electric)	30 nautical miles at 15.0 knots
	110 nautical miles at 10.0 knots
	170 nautical miles at 6.0 knots
	340 nautical miles at 5.0 knots
	490 nautical miles at 3.0 knots
Snorkel travel	9000 nautical miles at 8.0 knots
	16880 nautical miles at 6.0 knots

Diving Depth

Usual diving depth	133 meters
Normal fighting depth	220 meters
Destroying depth	330 meters

Armament

Torpedos six bow torpedo tubes,	533 mm (20 torpedos, or 14 torpedos + 12 TMC mines)
AA Guns	two 20 mm C/38 in twin mounts (inside bulletproof shields); 3450 rounds (originally planned 2 x 2 30 mm M 44)
Crew	6 officers (commander, LI, 2 WO, 1 WI, 1 BA), 5 NCO with, 14 without swordknot, 33 men,

total 58.

Only the tower of one of the Type XXI U-boats scuttled by their crews in Bremen at the end of the war is above the surface. The rear 20 mm twin Flak guns can be seen, also the already installed radar antenna.

These pictures were taken of the recovery, under Swedish
direction, of U 3503.
Above, the boat is seen lying on its side in a drydock.
Center, it is upright in a dock.
Below, the cut-open tower is seen.

Fate of the Type XXI U-boats, with dates and shipyards

Name	Shipyard	Keel laid	Launched	Put in service	Fate
U 2501	B & V	4/3/44	5/12/44	6/27/44	5/3/45 Hamburg S
U 2502	B & V	4/25/44	6/15/44	7/19/44	1/1/46 Operation Deadlight S
U 2503	B & V	5/2/44	6/29/44	8/1/44	5/4/45 n. of Fyn S
U 2504	B & V	5/20/44	7/18/44	8/12/44	5/3/45 Hamburg S
U 2505	B & V	5/23/44	7/27/44	11/7/44	5/3/45 Hamburg S
U 2506	B & V	5/29/44	8/21/44	8/31/44	1/1/46 Operation Deadlight S
U 2507	B & V	6/4/44	8/14/44	9/8/44	5/5/45 Geltinger Bucht S
U 2508	B & V	6/13/44	8/19/44	9/26/44	5/3/45 Kiel S
U 2509	B & V	6/17/44	8/27/44	9/21/44	4/8/45 Hamburg B
U 2510	B & V	7/5/44	8/29/44	9/27/44	5/2/45 Travemünde S
U 2511	B & V	7/7/44	9/2/44	9/29/44	1/2/46 Operation Deadlight S
U 2512	B & V	7/13/44	9/7/44	10/10/44	5/3/45 Eckernförde
U 2513	B & V	7/19/44	9/14/44	10/12/44	8/45 Given to USA
U 2514	B & V	7/24/44	9/17/44	10/17/44	4/8/45 Hamburg B
U 2515	B & V	7/28/44	9/22/44	10/19/44	1/17/45 Hamburg B
U 2516	B & V	8/3/44	9/27/44	10/24/44	4/9/45 Kiel B
U 2517	B & V	8/8/44	10/4/44	10/31/44	5/5/45 Geltinger Bucht A
U 2518	B & V	8/16/44	10/4/44	11/4/44	1951 Given to France
U 2519	B & V	8/24/44	10/13/44	11/15/44	5/3/45 Kiel S
U 2520	B & V	8/24/44	10/16/44	11/14/44	5/3/45 Kiel S
U 2521	B & V	8/31/44	10/18/44	11/21/44	5/4/45 s. of Flensburg (fireship) S
U 2522	B & V	8/28/44	10/22/44	11/22/44	5/5/45 Geltinger Bucht S
U 2523	B & V	9/6/44	10/25/44	12/26/44	1/17/45 Hamburg S
U 2524	B & V	9/6/44	10/30/45	1/16/45	5/3/45 s. of Fehmarn S
U 2525	B & V	9/13/44	10/30/44	12/12/44	5/5/45 Geltinger Bucht S
U 2526	B & V	9/16/44	11/30/44	12/15/44	5/2/45 Travemünde S
U 2527	B & V	9/20/44	11/30/44	12/23/44	5/2/45 Travemünde S
U 2528	B & V	9/25/44	11/18/44	12/9/44	5/2/45 Travemünde S
U 2529	B & V	9/29/44	11/18/44		2/22/45 Captured by Britain, given to USSR
U 2530	B & V	10/1/44	11/23/44	12/30/44	1/17/45 Hamburg B
U 2531	B & V	10/2/44	12/5/44	1/10/45	5/2/45 Travemünde S
U 2532	B & V	10/10/44	12/7/44	12/31/44	12/31/44 Hamburg B
U 2533	B & V	10/13/44	12/7/44	1/18/45	5/3/45 Travemünde S
U 2534	B & V	10/23/44	12/11/44	12/28/44	6/3-5/45 Göteborg B
U 2535	B & V	10/19/44	12/16/44	12/30/44	5/3/45 Travemünde S
U 2536	B & V	10/21/44	12/16/44	2/6/45	5/3/45 Travemünde S
U 2537	B & V	10/22/44	12/22/44	3/21/45	4/8/45 Hamburg B
U 2538	B & V	10/24/44	1/6/45	1/24/45	5/7/45 off Aerö S
U 2539	B & V	10/27/44	1/6/45	2/21/45	5/3/45 Kiel S
U 2540	B & V	10/28/44	1/13/45	2/4/45	5/4/45 s. of Flensburg (fireship) S
U 2541	B & V	10/31/44	1/13/45	3/1/45	5/5/45 Geltinger Bucht S
U 2542	B & V	11/13/44	1/22/45	2/10/45	4/3/45 Kiel B
U 2543	B & V	11/13/44	2/9/45	3/7/45	5/3/45 Kiel S
U 2544	B & V	11/15/44	2/9/45	3/10/45	5/5/45 near Aarhus S
U 2545	B & V	11/20/44	2/12/45	3/26/45	5/3/45 Kiel S
U 2546	B & V	11/22/44	2/19/45	3/21/45	5/3/45 Kiel S
U 2547	B & V	11/27/44	—	—	3/11/45 Hamburg B
U 2548	B & V	11/30/44	3/9/45	4/9/45	5/3/45 Kiel S
U 2549	B & V	12/3/44	—	—	— not finished
U 2550	B & V	12/5/44	—	—	— not finished
U 2551	B & V	12/8/44	3/31/45	4/-/45	5/5/45 Flensburg-Solitude S
U 2552	B & V	12/10/44	3/31/45	4/20/45	5/3/45 Kiel-Wik S
U 2553-64	B & V	—	—	—	— not finished
U 2565-2608	B & V	—	—	—	— not begun
U 2609-2643	B & V	—	—	—	— cancelled
U 2644-2762	B & V	—	—	—	— cancelled
U 3001	Deschimag	4/15/44	5/30/44	7/8/44	5/3/45 northwest of Wesermünde S
U 3002	Deschimag	5/23/44	7/9/44	8/6/44	5/2/45 Travemünde S
U 3003	Deschimag	5/27/44	7/18/45	8/22/44	4/4/45 Kiel B
U 3004	Deschimag	6/4/44	7/26/44	8/30/44	5/3/45 Hamburg S
U 3005	Deschimag	6/21/44	8/19/44	9/20/44	5/5/45 S
U 3006	Deschimag	6/12/44	8/25/44	10/5/44	5/1/45 Wilhelmshaven S
U 3007	Deschimag	7/9/44	9/4/44	10/22/44	2/24/45 Bremen B
U 3008	Deschimag	7/2/44	9/14/44	10/19/44	1945 to USA
U 3010	Deschimag	7/13/44	10/10/44	11/11/44	5/3/45 Kiel S
U 3011	Deschimag	8/14/44	10/20/22	12/21/44	5/3/45 Travemünde S

U 3012	Deschimag	8/26/44	10/13/44	12/4/44	5/3/45 Travemünde S
U 3013	Deschimag	8/18/44	10/19/44	11/22/44	5/3/45 Travemünde S
U 3014	Deschimag	8/28/44	10/25/44	12/17/44	5/3/45 Neustadt/Hol. S
U 3015	Deschimag	8/25/44	10/27/44	12/17/44	5/5/45 Geltinger Bucht S
U 3016	Deschimag	9/6/44	11/2/44	1/5/45	5/2/45 Travemünde S
U 3017	Deschimag	9/2/44	11/5/44	1/5/45	captured by British
U 3018	Deschimag	9/18/44	11/9/44	1/7/45	5/2/45 Travemünde S
U 3019	Deschimag	9/10/44	11/15/44	12/23/44	5/2/45 Travemünde S
U 3020	Deschimag	10/1/44	11/16/44	12/23/44	5/2/45 Travemünde S
U 3021	Deschimag	9/26/44	11/27/44	1/12/45	5/2/45 Travemünde S
U 3022	Deschimag	10/6/44	11/30/44	1/25/45	5/5/45 Geltinger Bucht S
U 3023	Deschimag	10/3/44	12/2/44	1/22/45	5/3/45 Travemünde S
U 3024	Deschimag	10/14/44	12/6/44	1/13/45	5/3/45 Neustadt/Hol. S
U 3025	Deschimag	10/12/44	12/9/44	1/20/45	5/3/45 Travemünde S
U 3026	Deschimag	10/19/44	12/14/44	1/22/45	5/3/45 Travemünde S
U 3027	Deschimag	10/18/44	12/18/44	1/25/45	5/3/45 Travemünde S
U 3028	Deschimag	10/26/44	12/22/44	1/27/45	5/3/45 Grosser Belt B
U 3029	Deschimag	10/24/44	12/28/44	2/5/45	5/3/45 off Kiel S
U 3030	Deschimag	11/2/44	12/31/44	2/14/45	5/3/45 e. Fredericia B
U 3031	Deschimag	10/30/44	1/6/45	2/28/45	5/3/45 Kiel-Wik S
U 3032	Deschimag	11/9/44	1/10/45	2/12/45	5/3/45 e. Fredericia B
U 3033	Deschimag	11/6/44	1/20/45	2/27/45	5/4/45 Wasserslebener Bucht S
U 3034	Deschimag	11/14/44	1/21/45	3/31/45	5/4/45 Wasserslebener Bucht S
U 3035	Deschimag	11/11/44	1/24/45	3/1/45	— to USSR
U 3036	Deschimag	11/22/44	1/27/45	—	3/31/45 Bremen B
U 3037	Deschimag	11/18/44	1/31/45	3/3/45	5/3/45 Travemünde S
U 3038	Deschimag	12/1/44	1/7/45	3/4/45	5/3/45 Kiel S
U 3039	Deschimag	11/29/44	2/14/45	3/8/45	5/3/45 Kiel S
U 3040	Deschimag	12/9/44	2/10/45	3/8/45	5/3/45 Kiel S
U 3041	Deschimag	12/7/44	2/13/45	3/10/45	— to USSR
U 3042	Deschimag	12/15/44	—	—	5/22/45 Bremen B
U 3043	Deschimag	12/14/44	—	—	— not finished
U 3044	Deschimag	12/21/44	3/1/45	3/27/45	5/5/45 Geltinger Bucht S
U 3045	Deschimag	12/29/44	3/10/45	—	3/30/45 Bremen B
U 3046	Deschimag	12/29/44	3/10/45	—	3/30/45 Bremen B
U 3047	Deschimag	1/3/45	4/11/45	—	5/5/45 Wesermünde S
U 3048	Deschimag	12/31/44	—	—	— not finished
U 3049	Deschimag	12/30/44	—	—	— not finished
U 3050	Deschimag	1/9/45	4/18/45	—	— w. Wesermünde S
U 3051	Deschimag	1/8/45	4/20/45	—	— w. Wesermünde S
U 3052-63	Deschimag	1945	—	—	— not finished
U 3064-88	Deschimag	—	—	—	— not begun
U 3089-3100	Deschimag	—	—	—	— cancelled
U 3101-76	Valentin	—	—	—	— not begun
U 3177-3295	Valentin	—	—	—	— cancelled
U 3501	Schichau	3/20/44	4/19/44	7/29/44	4/4/45 Wesermünde S
U 3502	Schichau	4/16/44	7/6/44	8/19/44	5/3/45 Hamburg S
U 3503	Schichau	5/12/44	7/27/44	9/9/44	5/8/45 off Göteborg, salvaged later
U 3504	Schichau	6/30/44	8/15/44	9/23/44	5/2/45 Wilhelmshaven
U 3505	Schichau	7/9/44	8/25/44	7/10/44	5/3/45 Kiel B
U 3506	Schichau	7/14/44	8/28/44	10/16/44	5/2/45 Hamburg S
U 3507	Schichau	7/19/44	9/16/44	10/19/44	5/3/45 Travemünde S
U 3508	Schichau	7/25/44	9/22/44	11/2/44	3/4/45 Wilhelmshaven B
U 3509	Schichau	7/29/44	9/27/44	1/29/45	5/3/45 Wesermünde S
U 3510	Schichau	8/6/44	10/4/44	11/11/44	5/5/45 Geltinger Bucht S
U 3511	Schichau	8/14/44	10/11/44	11/18/44	5/3/45 Travemünde S
U 3512	Schichau	8/15/44	10/11/44	11/27/44	4/8/45 Hamburg B
U 3513	Schichau	8/20/44	10/21/44	12/2/44	5/3/45 Travemünde S
U 3514	Schichau	8/21/44	10/21/44	12/9/44	1/3/46 Operation Deadlight S
U 3515	Schichau	8/27/44	11/4/44	12/14/44	— to USSR
U 3516	Schichau	8/28/44	11/4/44	12/18/44	5/2/45 Travemünde S
U 3517	Schichau	9/12/44	11/11/44	12/22/44	5/2/45 Travemünde S
U 3518	Schichau	9/12/44	11/11/44	12/29/44	5/3/45 Kiel S
U 3519	Schichau	9/19/44	11/23/44	1/6/45	3/2/45 n. Warnemünde by mine
U 3520	Schichau	9/20/44	11/23/44	1/12/45	1/31/45 Bülk by mine
U 3521	Schichau	9/-/44	12/3/44	1/14/45	5/2/45 Travemünde S
U 3522	Schichau	9/-/44	12/3/44	1/21/45	5/2/45 Travemünde S
U 3523	Schichau	10/-/44	12/14/44	1/29/45	5/5/45 off Aarhus B
U 3524	Schichau	10/-/44	12/14/44	1/26/45	5/5/45 Geltinger Bucht S
U 3525	Schichau	10/17/44	12/23/44	1/31/45	5/3/45 Kiel S

U 3526	Schichau	10/18/44	12/23/44	3/22/45	5/5/45 Geltinger Bucht S
U 3527	Schichau	10/25/44	1/10/45	3/10/45	5/5/45 Wesermünde S
U 3528	Schichau	10/26/44	1/10/45	3/18/45	5/5/45 Wesermünde S
U 3529	Schichau	11/2/44	1/26/45	3/22/45	5/5/45 Geltinger Bucht S
U 3530	Schichau	11/3/44	1/26/45	3/22/45	5/3/45 Kiel S
U 3531	Schichau	11/-/44	2/10/45	—	5/3/45 Travemünde S
U 3532	Schichau	11/-/44	2/10/45	—	5/5/45 near Brumsbüttelkoog S
U 3533	Schichau	11/16/44	2/-/45	—	after January-
U 3534	Schichau	11/17/44	2/-/45	—	February 1945 towed
U 3535	Schichau	11/26/44	2/-/45	—	to west, and broken
U 3536	Schichau	11/27/44	2/-/45	—	up after the end of
U 3537	Schichau	12/20/44	2/-/45	—	the war
U 3538	Schichau	12/21/44	2/-/45	—	
U 3539-42	Schichau	—	—	—	begun, not finished
U 3543-71	Schichau	—	—	—	not begun, some sections delivered
U 3572-74	Schichau	—	—	—	not begun
U 3575-3684	Schichau	—	—	—	contract postponed
U 3685-95	Schichau	—	—	—	contract canceled

These data were extracted from those in Rössler, Uboottype XXI (Koblenz 1986), the most thorough and reliable available to date. Abbreviations: A: lost in action, B: lost to enemy bombing; S: scuttled; e. east of; n. north of; s. south of; w. west of. Only the end result is noted here, regardless of previous events and later salvaging.
Shipyards: B & V: Blohm & Voss, Hamburg; Deschimag: Deutsche Schiffs- und Maschinenbau-Aktiengesellschaft "Weser", Bremen; Valentin: Bremer Vulkan Baubunker "Valentin", Bremen-Farge; Schichau: Friedrich Schichau-Werft, Danzig.

Three of the Type XXI German U-boats assembled at Lisahally, Scotland after the war ended and used in the "Deadlight" sinking action are seen here, from left to right, U 2502, U 3514 and U 2518.

"Childhood Illnesses" of the Type XXI U-boats

It could be seen from the beginning that in this new U-boat type that had been "created out of nothing" there would be difficulties and problems. These did in fact occur and were of the most varied types. For one thing, there were transport and delivery problems, originating from the shortage of materials and the frequent disturbance to transport routes by air raids, whether damage to supplier industries, lack of trained workers, materials or production machinery, or because means of transport had been destroyed or interrupted by air raids. All of this had to be accepted as resulting from the war, at least as long as it was possible to make do with improvisations. Other problems became evident only after the completion of the boats, and these were mainly of the technical type. There were watertightness problems with the pressure hull, the snorkel apparatus proved to be faulty, machinery and other components that required servicing or maintenance were hard to get at—these were just a few of the problems that occurred. These existed because the war situation no longer allowed building a prototype boat in which most problems would have been detected early enough to eliminate them from the production boats. The IBG began with the premise that these difficulties could be overcome because the first boats of the production series built at any shipyard would in any case have to be used for personnel training, so that all the experienced gained could be applied to series production.

Blohm & Voss 1944: The Author's Recollections

As of May 1944, my ship, the destroyer **Erich Steinbrinck**, lay in the shipyards of Blohm & Voss in Hamburg for a machinery overhaul that lasted several months. We had tied up here at the Steinwerder shore. At this time, U-boat construction was still going on at high speed. On the Elbe shore, between slipway groups 2 and 4 and the gigantic "Elbe 17" drydock, we spotted several small U-boats on land, set on blocks under camouflage nets and hard to recognize for what they were (they were—as it became known after the war—the so-called "Walter boats", which had been built for testing of their new power system, which was named after its inventor, Professor Walter and was being completed). They did not interest me very much, because one did not get to see very much of them and knew nothing else about them. On the other hand, the U-boat production on the large slipways nearby attracted my and my comrades' interest greatly: U-boats were growing there that obviously differed in shape and appearance from the previous boats and hinted at something new. More precisely, what one got to see was several stern sections that were being assembled—and every one of these separate parts was already—as could be seen clearly—completely set up and equipped. Soon I got to see the first completed boat of this series in its element: on May 12, 1944, around noon, I had received an order that I was to carry out at the administration building of the shipyard. My path led past slipways 9 and 10, where I saw a large number of "shipyard grandees" standing around doing nothing (which was otherwise very rare, since the "total war" was going on); obviously they were waiting for something. I stopped near them and asked the nearest of them if they were taking a break. His answer let me know that there was going to be something worth

seeing. And that is what happened: One of the new U-boats slid down the ways, completely without ceremony as was customary otherwise. But how that boat looked! A streamlined tower, a fully different stern, a much larger size than all the other U-boats that we had seen. Only after the war ended did I find out what I had gotten to see: the launch of the first Type XXI U-boat, U 2501, built by Blohm & Voss (the type classification was not known to us then; one spoke only of the "new U-boats"); it was the first of this type to be put into service. Naturally, I wanted to know what it amounted to—but several "shipyard grandees" whom I asked (that's what the shipyard workers were generally called by us Navy men) could or would say nothing, and so I turned to my division officer on "Z15", Oberleutnant z.S. v.R.-B., with whom I had a good relationship and who always listened to my questions. He probably didn't know too much about it either, but there was one thing I learned from him: that this boat was a new development that was meant for a new U-boat war. At this time there was a lot of talk about "new weapons" in the Nazi propaganda (the concept of a "wonder weapon", to my recollection, was used only after the attempt on Hitler's life on July 20). With that, the question was answered—very satisfactorily for me at that time—and I could not hope to learn more.

My interest in the new U-boat type did not die out; on the contrary, it kept growing steadily. Whenever my service allowed, my glances always turned toward the big slipways on which the new U-boats were being built. There was a constant change there, with sections arriving, being assembled, and boats being launched. As soon as one boat had slid into the water, it was only a matter of hours before pontoons brought in new sections that were pulled

The author remembers this event very well—on May 12, 1944, he watched the first launching of a Type XXI U-boat at Blohm & Voss, standing only a few meters from the site.

up the slipways by strong winches and lined up. Then the assembly began, and the whole process was repeated in continual sequence. Thus in the spring of 1944 I was a witness of at least eight to ten Type XXI launchings.

Work went on around the clock on the slipways. There appeared to be no interruptions. At this time the air raids on Hamburg began to increase, and the enemy—so it seemed to us—was concentrating on the shipyards. Not only was Blohm & Voss its target, but the nearby Deutsche Werft, Stülckenwerft and Howaldtswerke were also targeted. What surprised us "young marchers"—that was then the customary term for young soldiers—was that even under air-raid alarms, while all the personnel of the ships in the yards except those who were on guard duty were ordered into the air-raid shelters, work went on at the U-boat slipways! Only when things got really bad, when bombs fell, could the workers seek shelter in the nearby "pointed bunker" (so called because its top had a conical shape) or in a trench. This all had a ghostly effect in the night. The assembly by electric welding continued, making the usual shower of sparks. Of course measures were taken to cover them, as they would have been quite visible and have revealed the position, but it could not be completely prevented that the appearance of sparks got through to the outside and was even reflected much by the slipway framework. At this time there were many air raids of the Hamburg harbor area, but the deliberate massed bombings on the Type XXI production facilities began only after the end of the summer of 1944. And then they were really thick! Even so, the damage quota to sections and entire boats was quite meager at first; only after the end of the year did the air raids reach their high point, and then the destruction added up. What the workers accomplished then is hard to imagine today. The shipyard workers who built the U-boats worked under the roughest conditions, whether in summer heat or winter frost, always under the ever-growing danger of air raids, they did the hardest work to the last hour. Thanks to their efforts, the greatest U-boat program that there ever was could be carried out. I still can see the sight that I saw after the attack on the Blohm & Voss yards on November 4, 1944—the pictures of the workers who were killed, with their mortal remains looking so terrible that one might wonder how much worse it could get—and wish for the end of that horrible war. To this day I still have the highest respect for those "Werftgrandis". And there is another picture in my memory. On the day after the severe attack mentioned above, I saw a number of SS men on the shipyard grounds— although uniformed in field gray, they did not belong to the Waffen-SS but to the regular SS, which was responsible for security in the Reich. I was soon to find out why those men were at Blohm & Voss: Among the bombs that had fallen on the shipyards, there were several that had not exploded, some of them very close to the U-boat slipways. They had to be located and defused, for they blocked the further work on the Type XXI boats. To get at the unexploded bombs, they had to be shoveled out. This was done by men in striped outer clothing. At that time we thought they were regular prisoners; only later did it dawn on us that they were prisoners from a concentration camp (of the existence of which we knew). They had to dig until a fireman could get at the bombs to defuse them. When they had dug deep enough, the area was evacuated for some distance, and everyone had to go into the air-raid shelter. Thus we could not watch and see what became of the prisoners, but obviously they came to no harm, at least not that time, for none of the bombs blew up. But we were surprised; the prisoners dug and shoveled so devotedly that we noticed it. Did they just want to get it over with somehow? Or was their eagerness genuine, perhaps in hopes of avoiding being liquidated in camp? Were they Germans, foreigners, Jews? I never found out who they were or what became of them.

U 2501 after being launched. Right after its launching, the boat was taken in tow by tugboats and tied up at the central quay in the Blohm & Voss equipping harbor.

What Became of the Remaining Type XXI U-boats?

Each of the three victorious powers, according to an inter-allied agreement, received the right to take over some of the remaining Type XXI U-boats. Of the 123 boats put into service before the war ended, 23 had fallen victim to enemy aerial and naval attacks, 88 had been scuttled on orders, and only twelve were still afloat. Each of the victorious powers took some of them.

USA: Received U 2513 and U 3008; in August 1945 they were taken to a naval shipyard in Portsmouth, Virginia. As of 1947, both—without being put into service officially—were turned over to the Operational Development Force in Key West, Florida, where they were used in tests and experiments. The tower of U 3008 was rebuilt in the process; the 20 mm Flak guns were first removed from both boats. U 3008 was retired in the summer of 1948, U 2513 a year later. Both were used later as unmanned experimental objects. On October 7, 1951, U 2513 sank as a result of weapon action by the destroyer **Owens**; U 3008 went down in May 1952 after explosives tests.

Great Britain: The British took over only U 3017, which was designated N-41. It too was subjected to thoroughgoing design studies and tests. Shortly after it was taken over, there was an accident (battery explosion) on it. In November 1949 it was broken up at Newport.

Soviet Union: The Soviet Union received four units, as follows:

U 2529, taken over by the British at Kristiansand, Norway, in May 1945 and classified as N-28, assigned to the Soviet Union on November 5, 1945, registered in the fleet list as N-28 on February 13, 1946, used by the South Baltic Fleet from February 15, 1946 to September 24, 1955. On January 12, 1949 it was reclassified as a "large submarine" and renamed B-28 on June 9, 1949. On December 29, 1955 it was withdrawn from combat readiness and rebuilt as a stationary floating loading platform. On January 18, 1956 it was renamed PZS-34, withdrawn on March 25, 1958 and broken up.

U 3035: taken over by the British in Stavanger, Norway in May 1945 and classified as N-29, assigned to the Soviet Union on November 5, 1945 and registered in the fleet list as N-29, used by the South Baltic Fleet from February 15, 1946 to December 24, 1955, reclassified as a "large submarine" on January 12, 1949 and renamed B-29, withdrawn from combat readiness on December 29, 1955, and rebuilt as a stationary floating loading station, renamed PZS-31 on January 18, 1956, withdrawn on March 25, 1958, and broken up.

U 3041: taken over by the British at Horten, Norway in May 1945 and classified as N-30, assigned to the Soviet Union on November 5, 1945, registered in the fleet list as N-30 on February 12, 1946, used by the South Baltic Fleet from February 15, 1946 to December 24, 1955, renamed B-30 on June 9, 1949, withdrawn from combat readiness on December 29, 1955 and rebuilt as a

stationary floating loading station, renamed PZS 35 on January 18, 1956, reclassified as an experimental submarine on July 2, 1958 and simultaneously renamed B-100, withdrawn on September 25, 1959, broken up as of November 30, 1959.

U 3515: Taken over by the British at Horten, Norway in May 1945 and classified as N-30, assigned to the Soviet Union on November 5, 1955, registered in the fleet list as N-27 on February 13, 1946, used by the South Baltic Fleet from February 15, 1946 to December 24, 1955, withdrawn from combat readiness on June 10, 1955, renamed BSH-28 on September 19, 1955, rebuilt as a stationary floating training center, then renamed UTS-3 on January 9, 1957, withdrawn September 1, 1972, broken up as of February 5, 1973.

All the following U-boats were not, and in fact could not be, completed, and the appropriate Allied agreement stated in reference to captured warships that those which could not be completed within a time span of six months had to be eliminated as such. These units were found by the Soviets unfinished in the yards of the Schichau works in Danzig on March 30, 1945 and entered on the list of warships on April 12, 1945, given R numbers and assigned to the Baltic Fleet. They were all launched on July 15, 1945, but were not completed. As of March 8, 1947, they were given TS numbers (TS = Tsel, "target"). In the period of August 7-8, 1947 they were all sunk some 20 nautical miles northwest of Cape Ristna (Hiiumaa Island). They were dropped from the records on February 28, 1948. They were:
U 3538 (R-1, TS-5)   U 3539 (R-2, TS-6) U 3540 (R-3, TS-7)
U 3541 (R-4, TS-8)   U 3542 (R-5, TS-9)
The fate of the following boats was much the same, but they were never launched and were broken up at the shipyards:
U 3543 (R-6, TS-10) U 3544 (R-7, TS-11)
U 3545 (R-8, TS-12)

The same is true of these boats, which were never given R numbers and which were dropped from the records on April 9, 1947:
U 3546 (TS-13)   U 3547 (TS-15)   U 3548 (TS-17)
U 3549 (TS-18)   U 3550 (TS-19)   U 3551 (TS-32)
U 3552 (TS-33)   U 3553 (TS-34)   U 3554 (TS-35)
U 3555 (TS-36)   U 3556 (TS-37)   U 3557 (TS-38)

France: The French also gained the opportunity to get acquainted with a Type XXI U-boat. At the end of the war, the British had also acquired U 2518. This they assigned, at first as a loan, to the French. In February 1946 it was towed to Cherbourg, where it was put into service. On April 9, 1951 the boat was given the name **Roland Morrilot**, completing its final acquisition. The boat then remained in active service until being assigned to reserve status on April 15, 1967. It was sold for breaking up in 1969.

Finally, U 2540 must be mentioned. It was sunk in a bombing raid at Flensburg-Feuerschiff at the end of the war, and was raised under German supervision in 1957. In the autumn of 1958 it was turned over to the Howaldt Works at Kiel for repairs and restoration, so that the Bundesmarine could put it into service on September 1, 1960, under the name **Wilhelm Bauer** (NATO number Y 880). It spent its time of service exclusively as an experimental and test boat, and was taken out of service in 1983. In June 1983 it was obtained by the newly founded "Technikmuseum 'Wilhelm Bauer' e.V.". After being prepared and "demilitarized" by the Lloyd Works in Bremen, it was moored in the harbor of the Deutsches Schiffahrtsmuseum in Bremerhaven, and has been on display there since April 1984. This boat is the longest-lived of its type.

U 3503 was scuttled by its crew west of Göteborg on May 8, 1945. In 1946 the boat was raised by Sweden and broken up soon afterward. Here the crew is seen gathered on the upper deck shortly before the boat was scuttled.

Above: When this photo was taken, U 3515, its active service already behind it, had been taken by the Russian Navy. Here it is seen as UTS-3, a floating training station, as it was used from 1957 on.

Right: U 2540 just after it was raised in the summer of 1957.

*Below: U 2540, seen in 1961 as the test boat **Wilhelm Bauer**. The tower was modified in the course of its restoration.*

Could the War have been Won with the New U-boat?

This question has been asked repeatedly, but the answer can only be: No.Under the assumption that a sufficiently great number of well-developed Type XXI U-boats could have been ready for service at the right time, the U-boat war could have been brought to new life. The enemy defenses would have had a hard time with it: the previous means and methods of defense used by the ships (usually not fast enough) that escorted convoys would have failed against the fast U-boats that now operated underwater, and they could not be detected from the air by radar as long as they were under the surface. Thanks to their considerably improved capabilities, the new U-boats would once again have been capable of attacking convoys and sinking ships successfully. This would have forced the enemy to seek new ways of counteracting them. As long as that was the case, the Type XXI U-boats would at least have been able to cut down the tremendous stream of war materials of all kinds across the Atlantic, if not to halt it altogether, provided that their numbers were great enough. Their sinkings certainly would have been able to influence the war on the land fronts. Without these war materials, the Red Army certainly would have had a much harder job forcing the German troops to retreat out of the Soviet Union, and without the readiness of war materials and troops in Britain, it probably would have been all but impossible to carry out the invasion in the spring of 1944. The "Fortress of Europe" dominated by the Germans would have been able to hold off the enemy much longer.Such a development would not have stopped the Allies. If they had not been able to succeed on the sea or set foot on the Continent, then there would have been just one choice for them: The first atomic bombs would not have been dropped on Japan, but on targets in Germany, though it is uncertain whether the Germans would have surrendered as did the Japanese, who in the sumer of 1945 had been seriously weakened and had lost their military prospects.As long as the atomic bomb was not yet available, the Allies would have had to concentrate on new focal points for their strategic air warfare: U-boat shipyards, the fuel industry, supplying firms and the like would have become their primary targets. In their determination to destroy "Hitler's Germany", all the enemies agreed completely, thus it can scarcely be presumed that they would not have attained this goal. It would only have taken one or more years longer and led to even greater losses. The other side always had greater resources for waging war, while Germany's supplies sufficed for only a short period of time. From this perspective, the new U-boats could only have prolonged the war, for a decisive turnaround was no longer possible as of the middle of 1943 at the latest. No matter how successful the development of these new U-boats had been, they were doomed from the start by the words "Too late!"

The Type XXI U-boats were hunted when they—as seen here—came to the surface. This dramatic picture shows a Type XXI U-boat in the Skaggerak shortly before the war ended; it has been taken under fire by Allied aircraft. The bombs have struck dangerously close to the boat, which did not survive this attack.

The Historical Side
Ships Captured by the German Navy
3. Norwegian Minelayer Olav Trygvason

On the day of the occupation of Norway by the German Wehrmacht—on April 9, 1940—the minelayer **Olav Trygvason**, lying at the naval base at Horten, was taken and used as German spoils of war. The crew of the torpedo boat **Albatros**, which had been grounded and abandoned the next day in the course of these operations, was temporarily quartered on this ship, and on April 13 it was given that ship's name, **Albatros**. At first the naval leadership tolerated this, but after the artillery training ship **Brummer** had been lost after being hit by a torpedo from the British submarine **Sterlet** on April 14, 1940, they did away with the previous name. The former **Albatros** was renamed **Brummer**, following the principle that a loss suffered in direct action with the enemy deserved a higher status than one lost by accident. On May 11, 1940 it was put into service officially. In the ensuing time, the **Brummer**, now officially called a "mine ship", operated off the coasts of the Netherlands and Belgium, later in the eastern Baltic Sea, then along the Norse coast from the Skagerrak to Kirkenes and Petsamo, then back in the Skaggerak and the Baltic in 1944-45. Toward the end of the war it was at Kiel for a thorough overhaul at the the Deutsche Werke. On April 3, 1945, while lying in Dock 5, it was struck by bombs and badly damaged. During the cleaning-up work after the war ended, it was blown up and broken up in this dock.

This ship had been built at the Horten shipyards in Kiel in 1931, was launched on December 21, 1934 and put into service on June 21, 1934. It was designed as a minelayer, but in peacetime it was used as a cadet ship, as it had accommodations for 65 cadets. Its displacement was 1596 tons, according to the standard calculations, and 1924 tons when fully loaded for action, but without a load of mines. Its external dimensions were 92.52/97.30 meters in length at its design waterline and overall, 11.45 meters in width and 7.19 meters in lateral height; its draught, depending on its load, was 3.60 or 4.03 meters.

ts two propellers were powered by two DeLaval turbines with wheel drive; they received the required steam from three water-pipe boilers, each with 20 atmospheres of pressure. For marching and short trips, it could be powered by two eight-cylinder, four-stroke Sulzer Diesel engines. The turbines produced 6000 horsepower, the Diesel motors 1400 HP; with them, respectively, speeds of 22 and 19 knots could be attained. The fuel capacity including that of the required Diesel fuel was 200 tons. With it, a range of 3000 nautical miles at 14 knots was possible.

The armament consisted of four 12 cm SK L/45 guns (in single mounts with shields), one 76.2 mm Flak gun, and several small-caliber guns. Its armament also included four 45/7 cm torpedo tubes in two pairs, but these were seldom carried on board. The mine load amounted to sixty mines. Under German use, the 12 cm SK guns were replaced around 1941 by 12.7 cm SK L/45 guns, but the shields were unchanged. In 1943 the 12.7 cm SK guns in positions A, B and D were replaced by 10.5 cm SK L/45 gE guns, and the 12.7 cm SK in position C by light anti-aircraft weapons. In addition to the main artillery, there were ultimately two 3.7 cm L/83 C/38 Flak guns in single mounts, and up to ten 2 cm FlaMG C/30 and C/38 machine guns in various mounts. In all, 280 mines could be carried on board.

Only temporarily—probably only in 1940—did the **Brummer** carry disguising panels on both sides of its smokestack, meant to suggest a sloped funnel to make identification unsure. This was of little help, and the panels were removed soon afterward. The ship also had supports on its foremast and a radar device on the bridge.

*The **Brummer** (II) shortly after being taken over by the German Navy, but without modifications.*

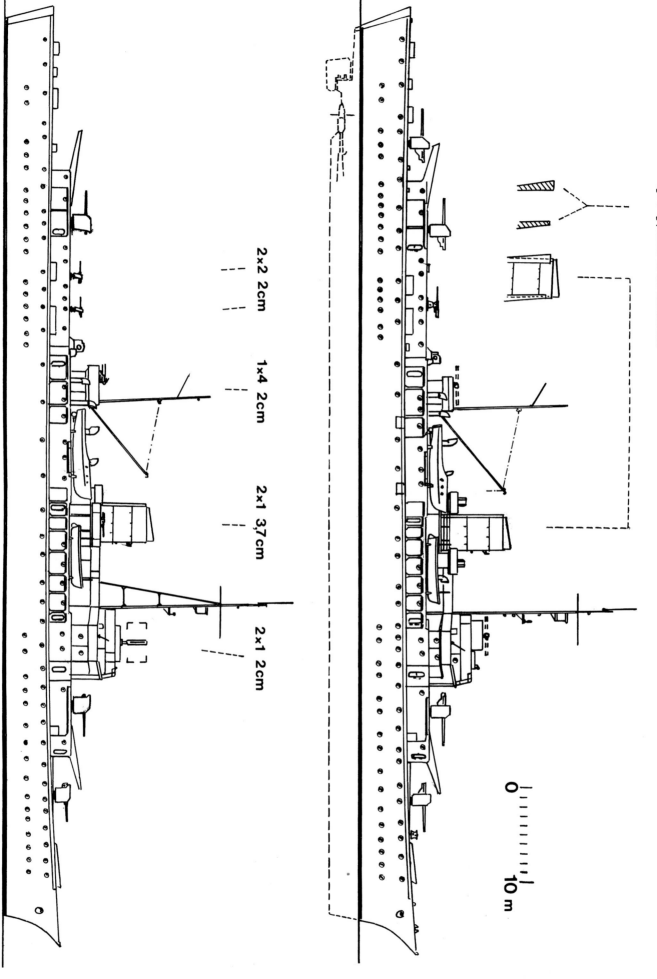

Disguising panels on the smokestack

2×2 2cm

1×4 2cm

2×1 3,7cm

2×1 2cm

0 .... 10 m

The **Brummer** (II), loaded with mines, in the Trondhjem Fjord in 1940. Disguising panels on both sides of the smokestack give the impression that the stack is tilted. This was to fool and annoy the enemy . . .

The forward guns of **Brummer** (II) . . .

. . . and the after guns. The old 12 cm guns, later replaced by German 10.5 cm types, can still be seen.

Brummer (II), circa 1941.

Brummer (II) in 1941, with camouflage paint.

Brummer (II) with different camouflage paint.

Brummer (II) in northern Norway in 1942, with three minesweepers of 1935.

Brummer (II) with different campuflage paint.

Brummer (II) with a load of mines, circa 1940-41.

The end of **Brummer** *(II): Lying in a drydock at the Deutsche Werke in Kiel, the boat was badly damaged in an air raid; shortly before the capitulation, explosions were set off, and the remains went the way of scrap iron.*

The Wreck of the Destroyer Georg Thiele (Z 2) Today

The bow of the German destroyer **Georg Thiele** (Z 2), after more than 45 years, still sticks out of the Rombaksfjord east of Narvik, where it was downed on April 13, 1940. A comparison with photos taken in 1940 shows that the bow has remained almost unchanged; only the first 12.7 cm gun was removed and the rear of the ammunition chambers was cut open in order to salvage the remaining ammunition. The force of the sinking can be seen clearly from the damage, the back deck is undamaged, the red and white paint is still visible on the capstan, the forwatd 12.7 cm gun is gone. The wreck can be reached only by boat or on foot; either one takes the train to Sildvik and gets out there (good walking shoes are recommended), or one goes by car along the road on the south shore of the Rombakfjord until it ends at a power station in a cavern. From there it is still about 1000 meters to the wreck, but there is no path.

The destroyer **Georg Thiele** (1934 type destroyer) was launched at the Deutsche Werke in Kiel on August 18, 1935 and put into service on February 27, 1937. It took part in Operation "Weserübung" for the occupation of Norway, within "Warship Group I", which had as its mission the occupation of the ore harbor of Narvik. For this the **Georg Thiele** had 200 mountain troops on board. During the first combat (with the 2nd British Destroyer Fleet) on the morning of April 10, 1940, the **Georg Thiele**, along with the **Bernd von Arnim** (Z 11), played a role in the sinking of the British destroyer **Hardy** and the damaging of its sister ship **Hunter**. But it also suffered seven direct hits, which knocked out the forward 12.7 cm gun, caused fires fore and aft, and killed thirteen crew members. During the second destroyer battle on April 13, 1940, the **Georg Thiele**, after the withdrawal into the Robaksfjord, placed itself crossways behind the Straumann Narrows to cover the scuttling of the destroyers **Hans Lüdemann** (Z 18), **Wolfgang Zenker** (Z 9) and **Bernd von Arnim** (Z 11). With its last torpedo, the **Georg Thiele** struck the British destroyer **Eskimo**, tearing away its bow up to the bridge. After its ammunition was used up, the wounded commander, Corvette Captain Wolff, drove his ship at full power onto the rocks on the south shore of the Rombaken. The crew disembarked; 27 of the men had been killed. After that the wreck was blown up and broke apart, leaving the bow lying on the rocks, where it can be seen to this day—like a warning monument.

Text and illustrations: Nikolaus Sifferlinger.

The arrow points to the wreck of the destroyer **Georg Thiele**.

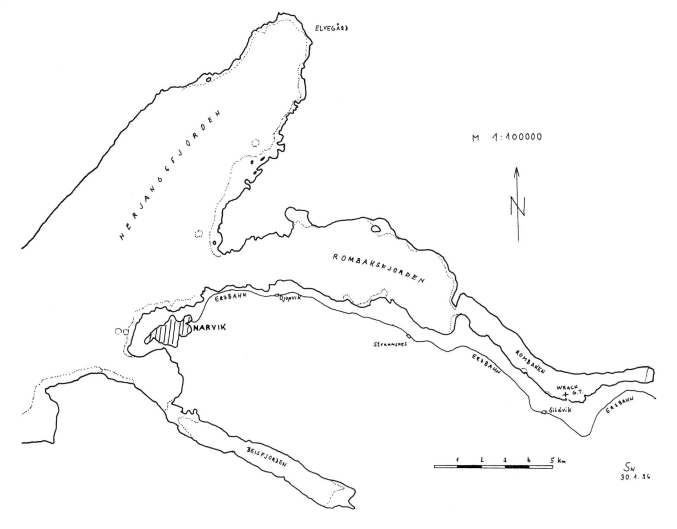

M 1:100000

N